MINDFUL MATH

Use Your GEOMETRY to Solve these Puzzling Pictures

Blackline Masters by Ann McNair

Illustrations by Robyn Djuritschek

Tarquin

PUBLISHER'S NOTE

Tarquin were delighted when Ann and Robyn approached us with the idea for the three books in this series. We have published and sold hundreds of thousands of copies of similar books for younger ages – see below – and had great success with other entertaining approaches to homework, revision and reinforcement. Books such as Mini Mathematical Murder Mysteries, Mathematical Team Games, Mathematical Treasure Hunts and Mathstraks activities – make up a wonderful set of resources for every style of learning and teaching.

The three Mindful Math titles join these books in our Tarquin eReader system, which allows you to add ebooks and then search for what you want so that you can print activities. We heavily discount ebook access for those who buy hard copy books, so they are as easy to use as possible.

See our full range at www.tarquingroup.com, sign up for our newsletters and follow us on Twitter and Facebook @tarquingroup for news, offers and new resources. All our books are available in the USA and Canada through www.ipgbook.com.

OTHER COLORING BOOKS FROM TARQUIN

Mindful Math – Algebra   ISBN 9781913565770
Mindful Math – Statistics   ISBN 9781913565794

For more coloring books for secondary ages, see the **By Design** series on our website

FOR AGES 5-11

Arithmetic Arithmetic   ISBN 9781899618149
The Multiplication Tables Colouring Book   ISBN 9780906212851
The Second Multiplication Tables Colouring Book ISBN 9781899618309

© 2021 Ann McNair and Robyn Djuritschek

Published by Tarquin Publications
Suite 74, 17 Holywell Hill
St Albans AL1 1DT, UK

www.tarquingroup.com

Distributed by IPG Books,
814 N. Franklin St.,
Chicago, IL 60610, USA

www.ipgbook.com

Design: Karl Hunt

Printed in the USA

ISBN (Book)   9781913565787
ISBN (EBook) 9781913565817

CONTENTS

1

MISSING ANGLES 1

(using simple angle facts)

PART 1: Calculate the missing angle *x*.

1.
135° *x*

2.
72° *x*

3.
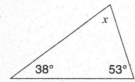
38°   53°   *x*

4.
41° 101° *x*

5.
56°
65°   *x*

PART 2: Calculate the missing angle *y*.

6.

y
140°
119°
40°

7.
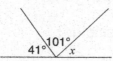
130°
y

8.

76°
y   82°

9.

y
110°
95°
85°

10.
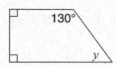
y
285°

PART 3: Calculate the missing angle *z*.

11.

z
62°

12.

z
70°   *z*

13.
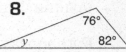
z

14.

55°
121°
z

15.
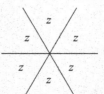
z
z   *z*
z   *z*
z

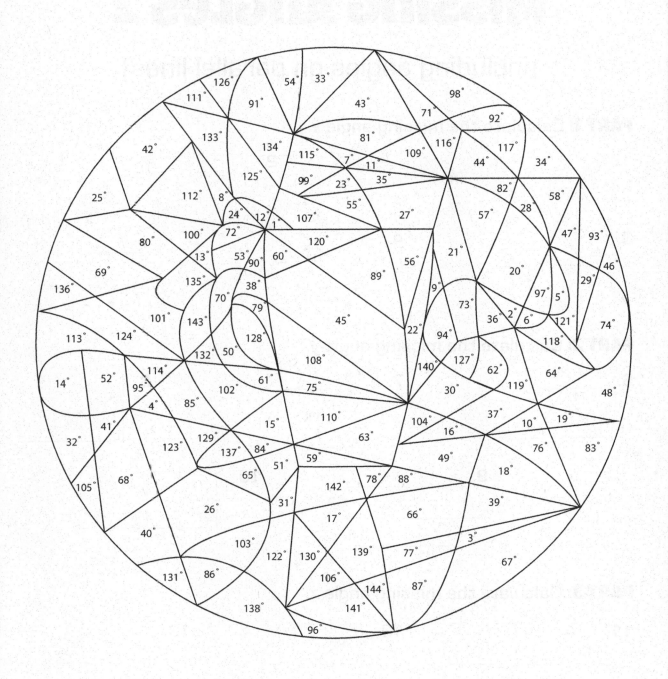

MISSING ANGLES 2

(including angles on parallel lines)

PART 1: Calculate the missing angle *x*.

1. 70° x

2. 52° x

3.  127° x

4. 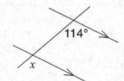 114° x

5. 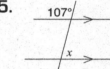 107° x

PART 2: Calculate the missing angle *y*.

6. 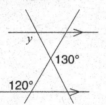 25° 74° y

7. y 130° 120°

8. 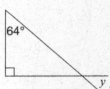 64° y

9. y 121°

10. y

PART 3: Calculate the missing angle *z*.

11. 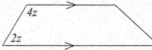 4z 2z

12. 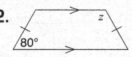 z 80°

13. 3z z

14. 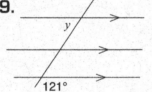 106° z 35°

15. 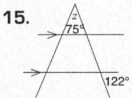 z 75° 122°

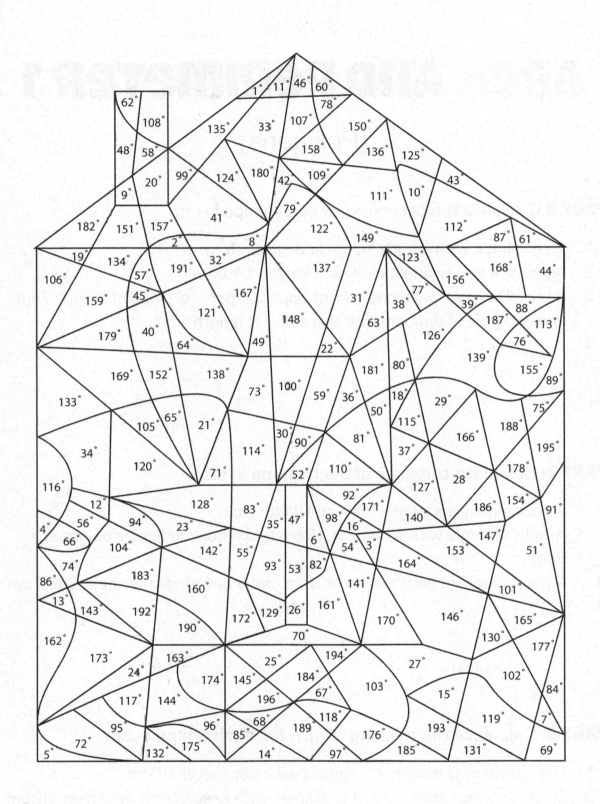

AREA AND PERIMETER 1

(Polygons)

PART 1: Calculate the perimeter of each shape in cm.

1. A rectangle with length 10cm and width 4cm.
2. An equilateral triangle with side length 14cm.
3. A parallelogram with one pair of opposite parallel sides of length 7cm and one pair of opposite parallel sides of length 5cm.

4.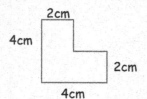

5.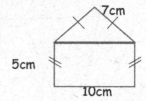

PART 2: Calculate the area of each shape in cm².

6. A rectangle with length 3cm and width 2cm.
7. A right triangle with a base of 12cm and a perpendicular height of 9cm.
8. A parallelogram with a base of 9cm and a perpendicular height of 7cm.

9.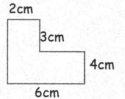

10.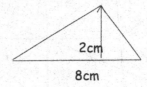

PART 3: Calculate the missing length for each shape in cm.

11. The length of the side of a square with perimeter 20cm.
12. The perpendicular height of a triangle with area 33cm² and base 22cm.
13. The short diagonal of a kite with area 216cm² and long diagonal 24cm.

Diagrams are not drawn to scale.

14.

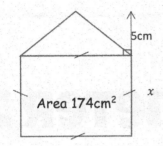

5cm

Area 174cm²

x

15.

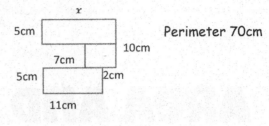

x

5cm

10cm

7cm

5cm   2cm

11cm

Perimeter 70cm

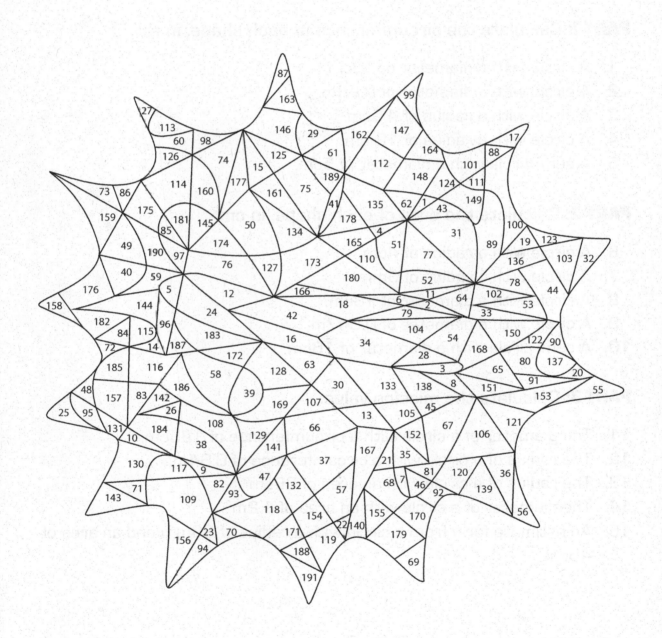

AREA AND PERIMETER 2

(circles)

PART 1: Calculate the circumference of each shape, in cm.

1. A circle with a diameter of 10cm.
2. A circle with a diameter of 0.26m.
3. A circle with a radius of 4.5cm.
4. A circle with a radius of 12mm.
5. A semi-circle with a diameter of 5cm.

PART 2: Calculate the area of each shape, in cm².

6. A circle with a radius of 4cm.
7. A circle with a radius of 8mm.
8. A circle with a diameter of 13cm.
9. A circle with a diameter of 0.047m.
10. A semi-circle with a diameter of 16cm.

PART 3: Calculate the missing value.

11. The diameter of a circle with a circumference of 125cm.
12. The radius of a circle with a circumference of 0.64m.
13. The radius of a circle with an area of 66cm².
14. The diameter of a circle with an area of 1.2m².
15. An estimate for π from a circle with a radius of 38mm and an area of 45cm².

Give answers to 1 decimal place.

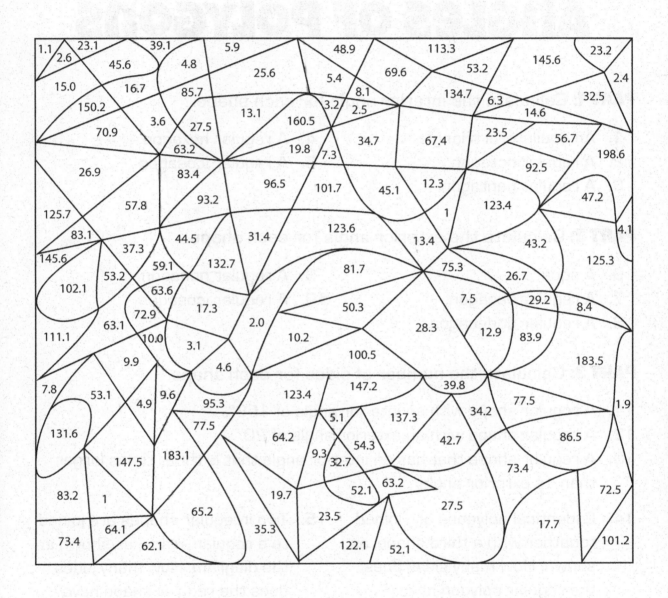

5

INTERIOR AND EXTERIOR ANGLES OF POLYGONS

PART 1: Calculate the interior angle for each shape.

1. An equilateral triangle.
2. A regular octagon.
3. A regular pentagon.

4. A regular hexagon
5. A regular icosagon.

PART 2: Calculate the exterior angle for each shape.

6. A square.
7. A regular decagon.
8. A regular dodecagon.

9. A regular nonagon
10. A regular icosagon.

PART 3: Calculate the number of sides for each shape.

11. A regular shape with an interior angle of 156°.
12. A regular shape with an exterior angle of 20°.
13. A regular shape that has an interior angle that is three times larger than its exterior angle.

14. 2 identical polygons are joined together with a third shape, as shown. How many sides does the regular polygon have?

15. Two irregular shapes are joined to a regular shape, as shown in the diagram. How many sides does the regular shape have?

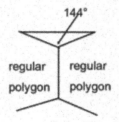

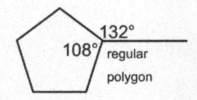

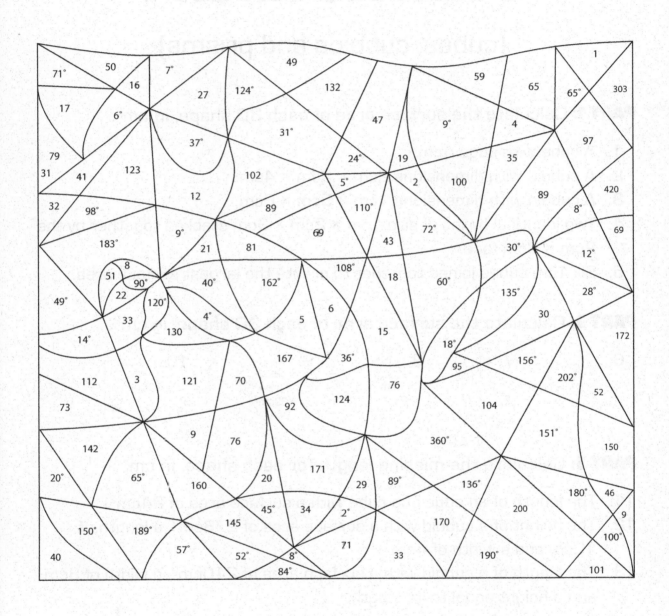

SURFACE AREA 1

(cubes, cuboids and prisms)

PART 1: Calculate the surface area of each 3D shape, in cm².

1. A cube with edge 4cm.
2. A cuboid with dimensions 2cm × 3cm × 4cm.
3. A cuboid with dimensions 1cm × 5cm × 6cm.
4. Two identical boxes of size 1cm × 2cm × 3cm stacked together by the 2cm × 3cm face.
5. Six 1cm cubes joined together to create the largest surface area.

PART 2: Calculate the surface area of each 3D shape, in cm².

6. 7. 8. 9. 10.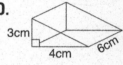

8. 6cm 7cm

9. area 39cm² 3cm 6cm

10. 3cm 4cm 6cm

PART 3: Calculate the missing length for each shape, in cm.

11. The length of an edge of a cube with a surface area of 24cm².
12. The height of a cuboid with a surface area of 276cm², a length of 10cm and a width of 4cm.
13. The length of a cuboid with a surface area of 210cm², a width of 8cm and a height equal to its length.
14. The length of an edge of the base of a square-based pyramid with a surface area of 275cm² and the area of each triangular face of 38.5cm².
15. How many cubes are lined up to make a surface area of 62cm²?

Diagrams are not drawn to scale.

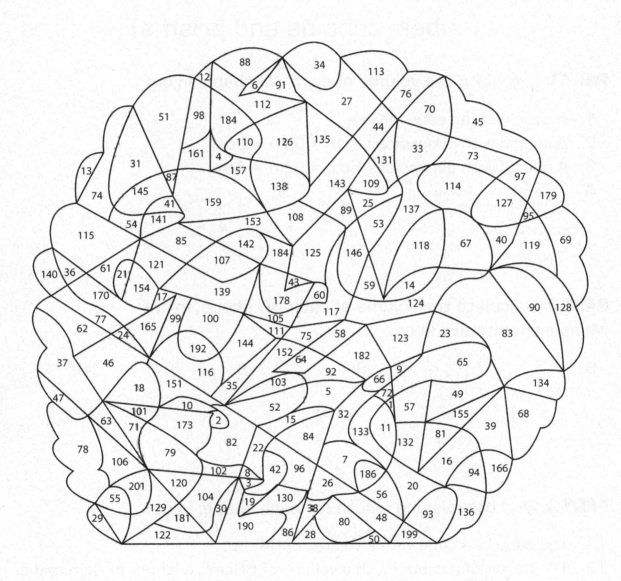

VOLUME 1

(cubes, cuboids and prisms)

PART 1: Calculate the volume of each 3D shape, in cm³.

1. A cube with an edge of 3cm.
2. A cuboid with dimensions 2cm × 3cm × 6cm.
3. A cuboid with dimensions 5cm × 5cm × 4cm.
4. 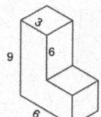 2cm cubes
5. 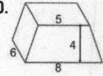 1cm cubes

PART 2: Calculate the volume of each 3D shape, in cm³. Measurements are in cm.

6.
7.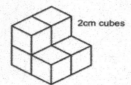
8.
9.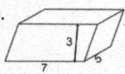
10.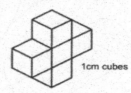

PART 3: Find the missing length for each shape, in cm.

11. The edge of a cube with a volume of 64cm³.
12. The height of a cuboid with a volume of 66cm³, a length of 4cm and a width of 5.5cm.
13. The length of a prism with a volume of 96cm³ and a cross-sectional area of 8cm².
14. The depth of the triangular prism shown, with a volume of 210cm³.
15. What is the length of the edge of a cube that has the same volume and surface area?

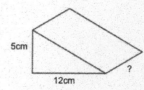

Diagrams are not drawn to scale.

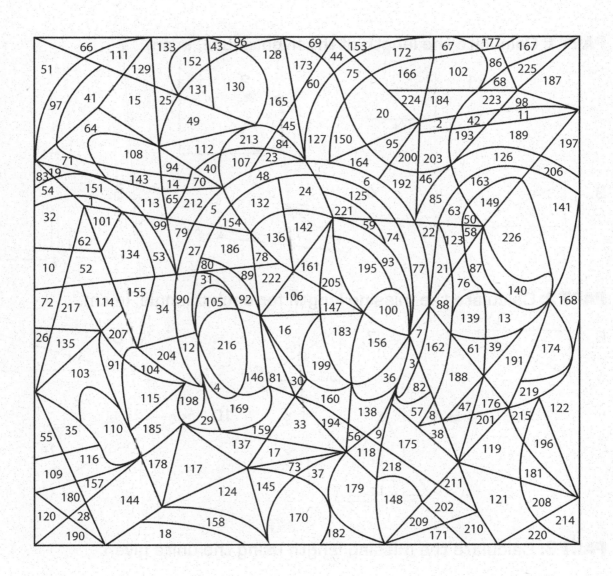

PYTHAGORAS' THEOREM

PART 1: Calculate the length of the hypotenuse, in cm.

1.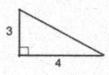
3
4

2.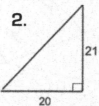
21
20

3.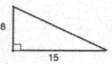
8
15

4.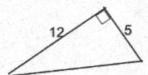
12   5

5.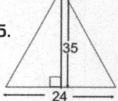
35
24

PART 2: Calculate the missing length for each triangle, in cm.

6.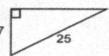
7   25

7.
6   10

8.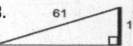
61   11

9.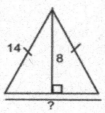
14   8   ?

10.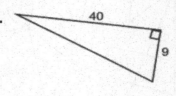
40   9

PART 3: Calculate the missing length using the units given.

11. A ladder 3m long is leant against a wall with a gap of 1m at the bottom. How far up the wall will the ladder reach?

12. A student starts at a point X on a level playing field. He walks 40m due east and then 16m due north. How far is he away from X now?

13. A rectangular gate of size 1.7m by 1.4m is strengthened by two diagonal struts. What length of wood is required for the two struts?

Diagrams are not drawn to scale. All measurements are in cm.

14. A 55 inch TV screen is 26 inches high. How wide is it?

15. What is the shortest distance between opposite diagonal corners (eg: top left corner to bottom right corner) of a cuboid of size 2.5m × 3m × 4.5m?

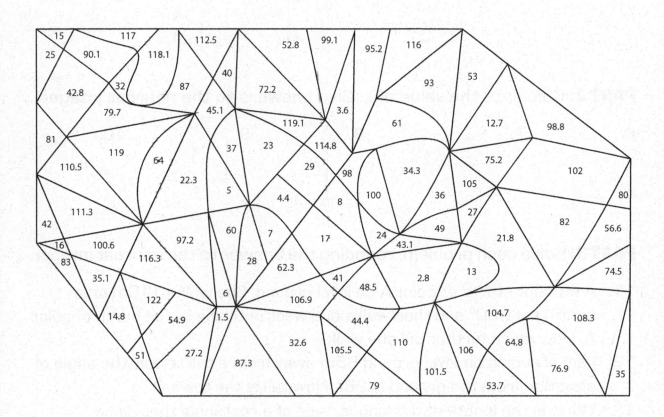

BASIC TRIGONOMETRY 1

(finding sides)

PART 1: Calculate the value of *x*. Give answers to the nearest whole number.

1.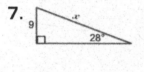
10
30°

2.
23
52°

3.
45°
8

4.
22
75°

5.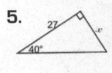
27
40°

PART 2: Calculate the value of *x*. Give answers to the nearest integer.

6.
21
45°

7.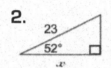
9
28°

8.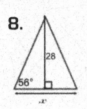
28
56°

9.
59°
32

10.
32.5
36°

PART 3: Solve each problem, rounding the answer to the nearest integer.

11. A student starts at point A on level ground. She walks 110m on a bearing of 060° and then walks due west until she is due north of point A. How much further did she walk?

12. I am standing on level ground 65m away from a tall tower. The angle of elevation from the ground is 36°. How tall is the tower?

13. What is the length of the longest side of a rectangle that has a diagonal of length 18cm that makes an angle of 64° with one of the edges of the rectangle?

14. A kite is flying 30m above level ground. At that moment the kite string makes an angle of 27° with the ground. How long is the kite string?

15. Calculate the perimeter of the triangle.

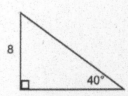
8
40°

Diagrams are not drawn to scale. All measurements are in cm for Parts 1 and 2.

10

BASIC TRIGONOMETRY 2

(finding angles)

PART 1: Calculate the missing angle, *x*.

1.

2.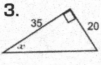

3.

4.

5.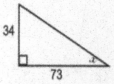

PART 2: Calculate the missing angle, *x*.

6.

7.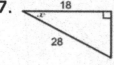

8.

9.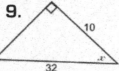

10.

PART 3: Solve each problem, rounding the answer to the nearest integer.

11.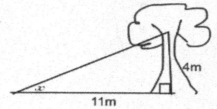

12.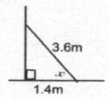

13. A road sign shows a hill with a gradient of 25%. What would be the angle of this hill?

14. A rectangle has a diagonal length of 12cm and a short side of 7cm. What angle does the long side make with the diagonal?

15. Calculate the angle of depression.

Diagrams are not drawn to scale. Give answers to the nearest whole number.

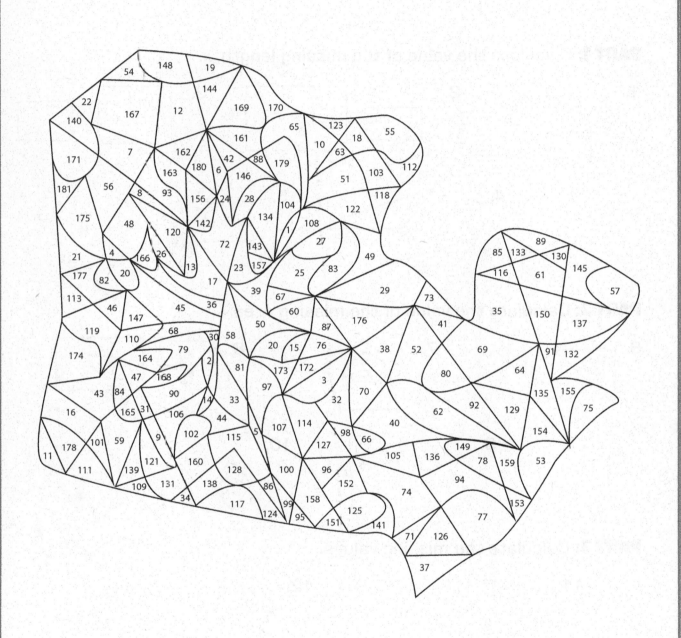

SIMILAR SHAPES

PART 1: Calculate the value of the missing length, *x*.

1.
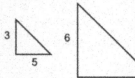

2.
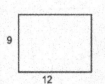

3.
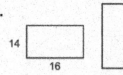

4.
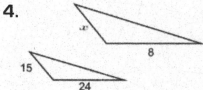

5.
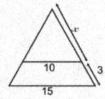

PART 2: Calculate the value of the missing area.

6.

7.

8.

9.

10.

PART 3: Calculate the missing values.

11.

12.

13.

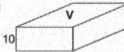

14.
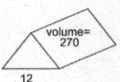

15.
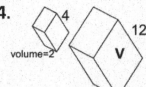

Diagrams are not drawn to scale.

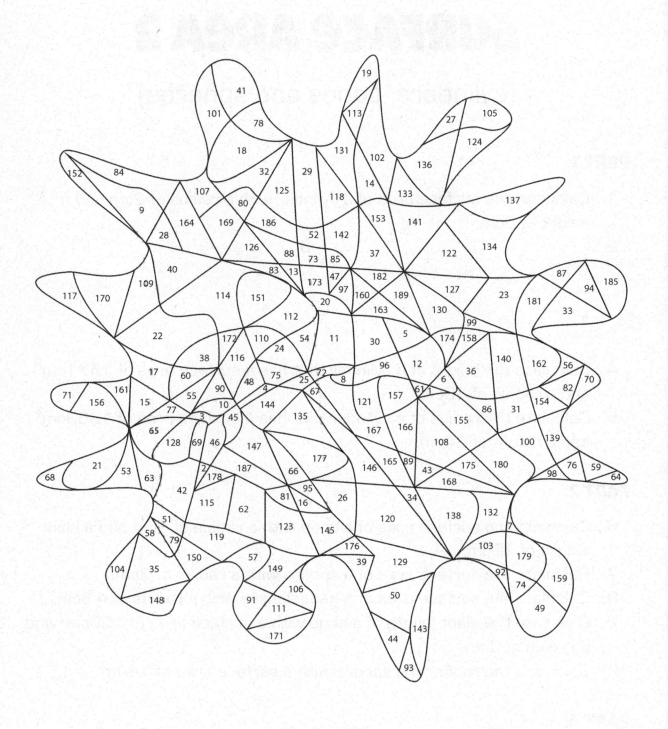

SURFACE AREA 2

(cylinders, cones and spheres)

PART 1:

1. Calculate the surface area of a cylinder with a radius of 2cm and a height of 5cm.

2.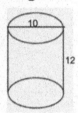

3.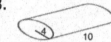

4. Calculate the height of a cylinder that has a surface area of 1571cm² and a radius of 10cm.

5. Calculate the radius of a cylinder that has a surface area of 1363cm² and a height of 24cm.

PART 2:

6. Calculate the surface area of a cone with a radius of 5cm and a slant length of 12cm.

7. Calculate the surface area of a sphere with a radius of 3cm.

8. Calculate the surface area of a hemi-sphere with a radius of 4.5cm.

9. Calculate the slant length of a cone with a surface area of 150cm² and a radius of 3cm.

10. Calculate the radius of a sphere with a surface area of 144π.

PART 3:

11. A round ball has a surface area of 113cm². Calculate its diameter.

12. A can of soup has a height of 11cm and a radius of 3.5cm. What is the area of the label if it has to include a 1cm overlap?

Diagrams are not drawn to scale. Give each answer to the nearest whole number.

Calculate the surface area of:

13. A cone and a hemisphere.

14. The lower frustum of the cone.

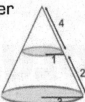

15. The capsule shown in the diagram made of a cylinder and two hemispheres.

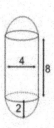

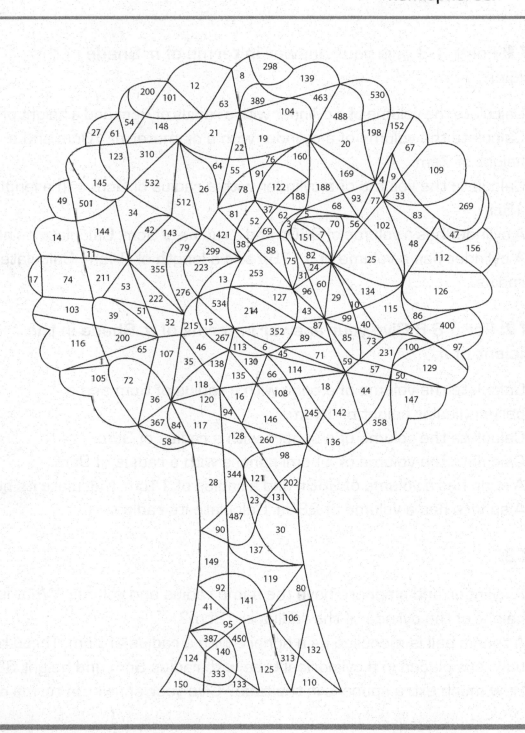

VOLUME 2

(cylinders, cones and spheres)

PART 1: For q 1-3 give your answer in terms of π. Shade in the coefficient of π.

1. Calculate the volume of a cylinder with a radius of 4cm and a height of 3cm.
2. Calculate the volume of a cylinder with a diameter of 10cm and a height of 7cm.
3. Calculate the volume of a cylinder with a radius of 3cm and a length of 15cm.
4. A cylinder has a volume of 960π and a radius of 8cm. Calculate its height.
5. A cylinder has a volume of 1176π and a length of 24cm. Calculate its radius.

PART 2: For q 6-8 Give your answer in terms of π. Shade in the coefficient of π.

6. Calculate the volume of a cone with a radius of 6cm and a perpendicular height of 13cm.
7. Calculate the volume of a sphere with a radius of 3cm.
8. Calculate the volume of a hemi-sphere with a radius of 9cm.
9. A cone has a volume of 968π and a radius of 11cm. Calculate its height.
10. A sphere has a volume of 288π. Calculate its radius.

PART 3:

11. A cylinder and a sphere have the same radius and volume. What is the height of the cylinder if the radius is 12cm?
12. A tennis ball is modelled as a sphere with a radius of 6cm. Three tennis balls are placed in a cylindrical tube with radius 6cm and height 38cm. How much extra space is in the tube? Give your answer in terms of π.

13. A sphere is found to have its volume equal to its surface area. What is its radius?

14. The three spherical metal balls of radii 5cm, 5.5cm and 6cm are melted down and formed into a new spherical metal ball. What will its radius be?

15. A solid cone with a base radius of 5cm and a perpendicular height of 17cm is made from a material with a density of $8.7g/cm^3$. Find the mass of the cone to the nearest kg.

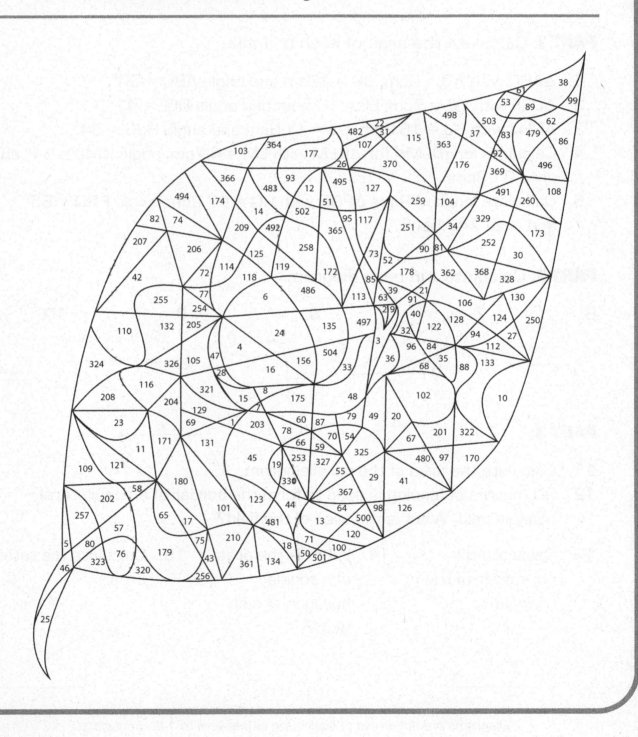

AREA OF A TRIANGLE

(not a right triangle)

PART 1: Calculate the area of each triangle.

1. ΔABC with AB = 6cm, BC = 10cm and angle ABC = 30°.
2. ΔDEF with DE = 7cm, EF = 13.5cm and angle DEF = 47°.
3. ΔGHJ with HJ = 16.2cm, GJ = 11.6cm and angle HJG = 84°.
4. Calculate length MK for ΔKLM with LM = 4.7cm, angle KML = 64° and area 21.3cm².
5. Calculate length PR for ΔPQR with RQ = 17.2cm, angle PRQ = 65° and area 747.5cm².

PART 2: Calculate x in each diagram.

6.

74° x
24
area=180

7.

x
area=33.4
121°
13

8.

x
area=76.7
65°
14

9.

8
area=15.6
x
9

10.

x
11
area=47.3

PART 3:

12
55°
5

11. Calculate the area of the parallelogram.
12. 90 metres of fencing is used to form the border of an equilateral triangle field. What is the area of the field?

13. Calculate the perimeter of the triangle.

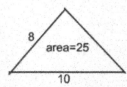

8
area=25
10

14. What is the area of a regular hexagon of side 8cm?

15. Calculate the total area.

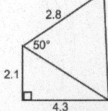

2.8
50°
2.1
4.3

Diagrams are not drawn to scale. Give all answers to 1 decimal place.

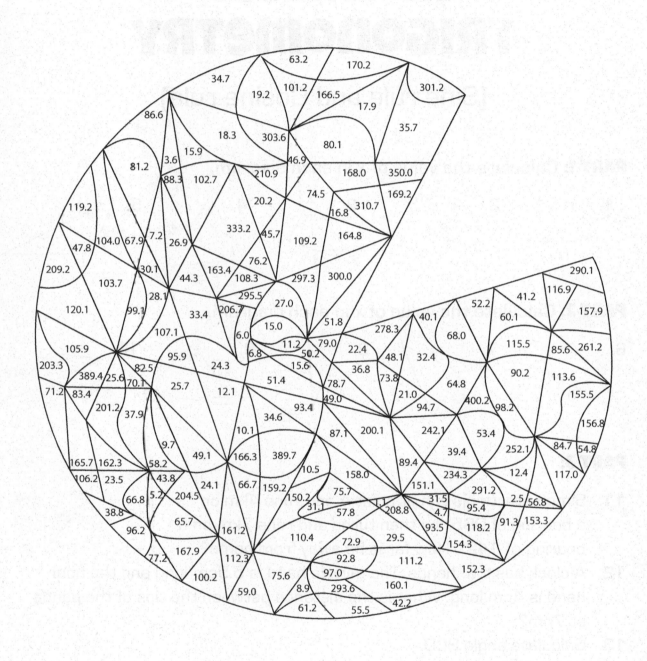

15

ADVANCED TRIGONOMETRY

(Sine rule and Cosine rule)

PART 1: Calculate the value of *x* in each diagram.

1.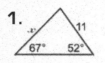

2.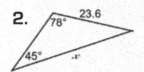

3.

4.

5.

PART 2: Calculate the value of *x* in each diagram.

6.

7.

8.

9.

10.

PART 3:

11. Simon starts his run at point A and runs 4km on a bearing of 065° he then turns and runs 7km on a bearing of 142°. How far is he away from home?

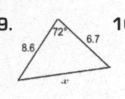

12. A clock has two hands. The minute hand is 5.5cm long and the hour hand is 4cm long. What is the distance between the tips of the hands at 7pm?

13. Calculate angle BCD.

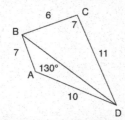

Diagrams are not drawn to scale. Give all answers to 1 decimal place.

14. A hot air balloon is tethered to the ground at points A and B. Calculate the angle of elevation at point A.

15. Calculate the height above the ground of the balloon, using the rounded answer from q14.

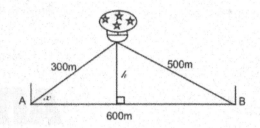

Answers

1. MISSING ANGLES 1

Part 1: 45, 108, 89, 38, 59

Part 2: 61, 50, 22, 70, 75

Part 3: 56, 110, 120, 63, 60

2. MISSING ANGLES 2

Part 1: 70, 52, 53, 114, 73

Part 2: 81, 110, 26, 59, 90

Part 3: 30, 100, 36, 71, 47

3. AREA AND PERIMETER 1

Part 1: 28, 42, 24, 16, 34

Part 2: 6, 54, 63, 30, 8

Part 3: 5, 3, 18, 12, 13

4. AREA AND PERIMETER 2

Part 1: 31.4, 81.7, 28.3, 7.5, 12.9

Part 2: 50.3, 2.0, 132.7, 17.3, 100.5

Part 3: 39.8, 10.2, 4.6, 123.6, 3.1

5. INTERIOR AND EXTERIOR ANGLES

Part 1: 60°, 135°, 108°, 120°, 162°

Part 2: 90°, 36°, 30°, 40°, 18°

Part 3: 15, 18, 8, 5, 6

6. SURFACE AREA 1

Part 1: 96, 52, 82, 32, 26

Part 2: 42, 22, 133, 186, 84

Part 3: 2, 7, 5, 11, 15

7. VOLUME 1

Part 1: 27, 36, 100, 48, 5

Part 2: 90, 216, 77, 105, 156

Part 3: 4, 3, 12, 7, 6

8. PYTHAGORAS' THEOREM

Part 1: 5, 29, 17, 13, 37

Part 2: 24, 8, 60, 23, 41

Part 3: 2.8, 43.1, 4.4, 48.5, 6

9. BASIC TRIGONOMETRY 1

Part 1: 5, 14, 8, 6, 23

Part 2: 21, 19, 38, 62, 55

Part 3: 95, 47, 16, 66, 30

10. BASIC TRIGONOMETRY 2

Part 1: 45, 68, 30, 39, 25

Part 2: 79, 50, 23, 72, 17

Part 3: 20, 67, 14, 36, 58

11. SIMILAR SHAPES

Part 1: 10, 48, 8, 5, 6

Part 2: 11, 45, 24, 20, 75

Part 3: 96, 4, 12, 54, 30

12. SURFACE AREA 2

Part 1: 88, 534, 352, 15, 7

Part 2: 267, 113, 127, 13, 6

Part 3: 3, 253, 214, 75, 151

13. VOLUME 2

Part 1: 48, 175, 135, 15, 7

Part 2: 156, 36, 486, 24, 6

Part 3: 16, 504, 3, 8, 4

14. AREA OF A TRIANGLE

Part 1: 15.0, 34.6, 93.4, 10.1, 95.9

Part 2: 15.6, 6.0, 12.1, 25.7, 51.4

Part 3: 49.1, 389.7, 24.3, 166.3, 9.7

15. ADVANCED TRIGONOMETRY

Part 1: 9.4, 32.6, 14.9, 67.3, 143.8

Part 2: 43.5, 41.3, 133.2, 9.1, 88.7

Part 3: 8.8, 9.2, 149.0, 56.3, 249.6

SOLVED PUZZLES

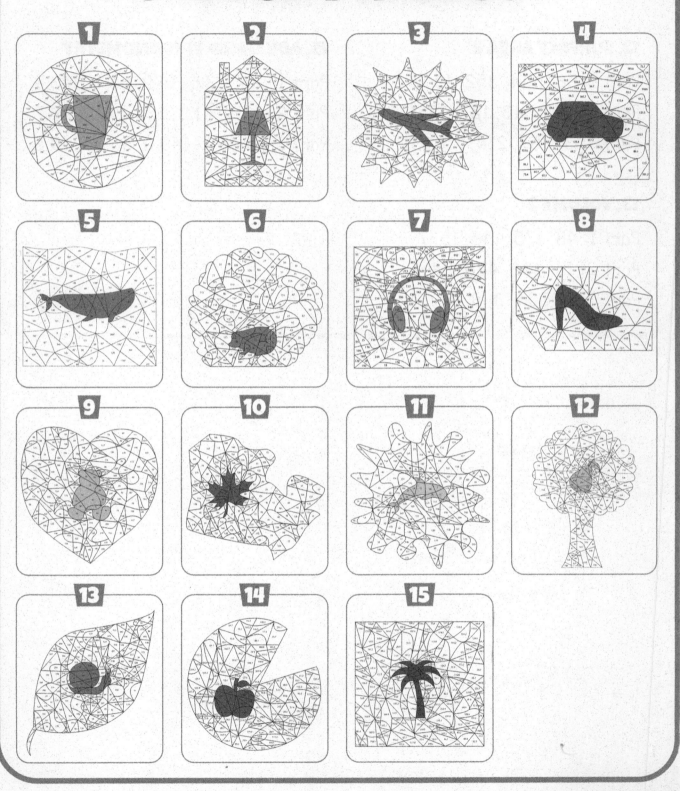

MINDFUL MATH

Use Your Geometry to Solve these Puzzling Pictures

Destress your math practice with this classic Tarquin format that has now been used to teach millions of students.

This book provides a restful way for those learning geometry to revise and reinforce their skills by solving the questions correctly and shading the answers – thus revealing the answer to the puzzle picture.

15 activities cover topics such as:

- Missing Angles – angle facts
- Area and Perimeter (circles and polygons)
- Interior and Exterior Angles of Polygons
- Surface Area 1 (cubes, cuboids, prisms, cylinders, cones and spheres)
- Volume (cubes, cuboids, prisms, cylinders, cones and spheres)

- Pythagoras' Theorem
- Trigonometry (finding sides, finding angles, the Sine and Cosine rule)
- Similar Shapes
- Area of a non-right triangle

Parents, teachers and students will love them.

Fun to use – and self-marking too.

There are two more volumes in the Mindful Math series – full details inside.

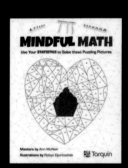

Blackline Masters by **Ann McNair**

Illustrations by **Robyn Djuritschek**

ISBN 978-1-913565-78-7   US$7.99

9 781913 565787

Tarquin

MINDFUL MATH

$x + 42 = 113$ $5x = 100$ $x + 3 = 10$

Use Your ALGEBRA to Solve these Puzzling Pictures

Masters by Ann McNair

Illustrations by Robyn Djuritschek

 Tarquin